COOL
PLASTIC BOTTLE
SCIENCE

BY TAMMY ENZ

Consultant:
Marcelle A. Siegel
Associate Professor of Science Education
University of Missouri, Missouri, USA

raintree

Raintree is an imprint of Capstone Global Library Limited, a company incorporated in England and Wales having its registered office at 264 Banbury Road, Oxford, OX2 7DY – Registered company number: 6695582

www.raintree.co.uk
myorders@raintree.co.uk

Text © Capstone Global Library Limited 2017
The moral rights of the proprietor have been asserted.

ted by Brenda Haugen
ned by Russell Griesmer
esearch by Tracey Cummins
ction by Kathy McColley
nated by Capstone Press
ted and bound in China

8 1 4747 2197 4 (hardback)
20 19 18 17 16
0 9 8 7 6 5 4 3 2 1

ISBN 978 1 4747 2201 8 (paperback)
21 20 19 18 17
10 9 8 7 6 5 4 3 2 1

British Library Cataloguing in Publication Data
A full catalogue record for this book is available from the British Library.

Acknowledgements
We would like to thank the following for permission to reproduce photographs: Capstone Studio: Karon Dubke. Design elements provided by Shutterstock: bimka, FINDEEP, fourb, Golbay, jannoon028, mexrix, Picsfive, Sarunyu_foto, STILLFX, Your Design

Every effort has been made to contact copyright holders of material reproduced in this book. Any omissions will be rectified in subsequent printings if notice is given to the publisher.

All the internet addresses (URLs) given in this book were valid at the time of going to press. However, due to the dynamic nature of the internet, some addresses may have changed, or sites may have changed or ceased to exist since publication. While the author and publisher regret any inconvenience this may cause readers, no responsibility for any such changes can be accepted by either the author or the publisher.

CONTENTS

COOL PLASTIC
BOTTLE SCIENCE

PLASTIC WITH PURPOSE

Milk, water, juice, pop — it seems like every drink comes in a plastic bottle. When you're done quenching your thirst, where do those bottles go? And where do they come from in the first place? Learn the answers to these questions and more. Then check out exciting ways to repurpose bottles into cool science experiments. Dig into your recycling bin, and get started.

GREAT PACIFIC GARBAGE PATCH

Plastic bottles are useful and durable. However, if not recycled they often end up in the Great Pacific Garbage Patch. Some scientists think this patch could be six times the size of the UK. Ocean currents trap rubbish dumped on land and in the waters of Asia and North America. Bottles can spend years floating in this rubbish patch, breaking down into tiny pieces called microplastics. Sea animals often mistake plastic pieces for food. Eating plastic can kill them.

CLOUD IN A BOTTLE

Seeing a cloud in the sky might not seem remarkable. But there's a recipe for making clouds. Meet all the conditions, and you can whip one up in your kitchen!

BRANCH OF SCIENCE: EARTH SCIENCE
CONCEPT: CLOUD FORMATION

YOU'LL NEED:

- Clean, empty 2-litre pop bottle with cap
- Water
- Dark sheet of sugar paper
- Torch
- Matches
- A friend

PUT IT TOGETHER:

STEP 1: Fill the bottom of the bottle with about 2.5 centimetres (1 inch) of water. Screw on the cap. Shake the water around in the bottle.

STEP 2: Prop the sugar paper against a wall. Place the bottle in front of it. Squeeze it tightly. Let go.

STEP 3: As you let go, ask a friend to shine the torch into the bottle. Do you see a cloud?

STEP 4

STEP 4: Ask an adult to light two matches at the same time. Uncap the bottle, and drop the matches in the water. Quickly replace the cap.

STEP 5: Shake the bottle, and place it against the paper.

STEP 6: Squeeze the bottle tightly, and let it go while a friend shines light on the bottle. For a few seconds you will see a cloud appear.

STEP 7: Repeatedly squeeze the bottle to see the cloud form again and again.

REUSABLE KNOWLEDGE:

By shaking the bottle, you filled it with water vapour. Squeezing the bottle increased the air pressure and the temperature. Releasing the bottle decreased the air pressure and lowered the temperature. Cooling water vapour formed droplets, which clung to the smoke inside. When these three things happen in the atmosphere, clouds form. Dust, smoke or volcanic ash in the air help out.

FAST FACT:

Bottles and many plastic packages are made from polyethylene terephthalate (PET). PET is a strong lightweight plastic. Its long chains of repeating molecules make it easy to form. Carbon dioxide can't seep through PET, making it ideal for pop bottles.

water vapour   water in its gaseous state

atmosphere   layer of gases surrounding Earth

MILK BOTTLE SIPHON

Think you can get water to flow uphill? How about keeping it flowing to drain a bottle dry? You bet. It's easy to do and fun to watch again and again with this experiment.

BRANCH OF SCIENCE: EARTH SCIENCE
CONCEPT: ATMOSPHERIC PRESSURE

YOU'LL NEED:

- 2 clean, empty milk bottles
- Food colouring (any colour)
- 2.5–3 metres (8–10 feet) clean, clear plastic hose

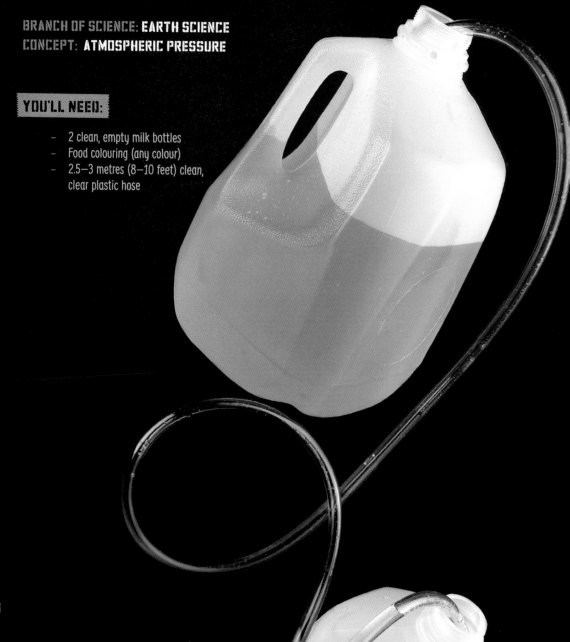

PUT IT TOGETHER:

STEP 1: Fill one bottle with tap water. Add several drops of food colouring.

STEP 2: Place this bottle on a table or counter.

STEP 3: Place the other bottle on the floor nearby.

STEP 4: Insert the hose into the top bottle. Push it all the way in. Make sure its end is near the bottom of the bottle.

STEP 5: Place the other end of the hose near the bottom bottle. Include some loops in the hose.

STEP 6: Gently suck on the bottom end of the hose. As the water nears your mouth, quickly stick the end inside the bottom bottle. What happens?

STEP 6

REUSABLE KNOWLEDGE:

Did you realize that the air around you is constantly pushing on you? This pressure is called atmospheric pressure. It's what makes a siphon work. Sucking air out of the tube decreases the pressure inside. This causes atmospheric pressure to push water into the tube. As the water moves through the tube, its pressure is lowered again. Atmospheric pressure keeps pushing until the bottle is dry.

RECYCLING PLASTIC MILK BOTTLES

Plastic milk bottles are recycled into soap dispensers, garden products and plastic 'wood' planks. 3D printers even use old milk bottles for printing material. Why not use old milk bottles to make more milk bottles? Used bottles could contain impurities, making them unsafe for food packaging.

atmospheric pressure   pressure caused by the weight of the atmosphere

CARTESIAN DIVER

Your command of this little diver will amaze you. You can thank the properties of gases for this experiment.

BRANCH OF SCIENCE: CHEMISTRY
CONCEPT: BOYLE'S LAW

YOU'LL NEED:

- Clean, empty 2-litre pop bottle with cap
- Ruler
- Water
- Small sauce packet

PUT IT TOGETHER:

STEP 1: Fill the bottle with water to within 5 centimetres (2 inches) of the top.

STEP 2: Drop a sauce packet into the bottle. Make sure it floats just below the water. Experiment with several packets until you find one that works.

STEP 3: Screw the cap on the bottle.

STEP 4: Squeeze the bottle. What happens?

STEP 5: Let it go. What happens now?

REUSABLE KNOWLEDGE:

An air pocket inside the packet keeps it light enough to float. When you squeeze the bottle, the air pocket becomes smaller. Now the "diver" sinks. This marvel is explained by Boyle's Law. Boyle's Law states that increasing pressure will decrease volume and vice versa.

FAST FACT:

Water is very heavy. It weighs 1,025 kilograms per cubic metre (64 pounds per cubic foot). The deeper a diver goes under water, the more pressure he feels. Deep-water divers cannot breathe because of the pressure on their lungs. Pressurized air from a SCUBA tank gives lungs enough pressure to combat water pressure. SCUBA stands for Self-Contained Underwater Breathing Apparatus.

UPSIDE DOWN WATER

Water can easily flow through a mesh window screen, right? Not so fast! In this experiment water does the unthinkable.

YOU'LL NEED:

- Clean, empty milk bottle
- Water
- 15-centimetre (6-inch) square of mesh window screen
- Rubber band
- Several toothpicks
- A friend

PUT IT TOGETHER:

STEP 1: Add water to the bottle until it's 1/3 full.

STEP 2: Place the screen over the opening in the bottle. Wrap the rubber band around the screen to hold it to the neck of the milk bottle.

STEP 3: Outside or over a sink, carefully turn the bottle upside down. Hold on to the bottle's handle.

STEP 4: Steady the bottle while holding the handle. Make sure not to squeeze it. What happens?

STEP 5: Ask a friend to carefully push a toothpick through a hole in the screen. What happens?

STEP 2

REUSABLE KNOWLEDGE:

Water molecules are strongly attracted to one another. This attraction is called cohesion.
Under water's surface, molecules are attracted equally in all directions. This attraction
is unequal at the water's surface. Here water molecules are attracted inwards only. So
molecules act like a thin elastic skin where they meet air. We call this surface tension.
This skin stretches across the screen holes. It holds water inside the bottle.

molecule   smallest particle of a substance with the properties of that substance

cohesion   ability to stick together

surface tension   water 'skin'; water molecules form stronger bonds at the surface,
causing the surface to act like a membrane

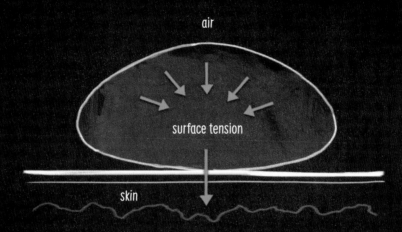

air

surface tension

skin

A WATERY SKIN

Surface tension acts like a skin on water's surface. Small drops of liquid
are spherical because cohesion pulls the molecules inwards.

BALLOON INFLATOR

Blowing up balloons can wear out your lungs. Let something else do the work. A little chemical reaction is all it takes.

BRANCH OF SCIENCE: CHEMISTRY
CONCEPT: ACID/BASE REACTION

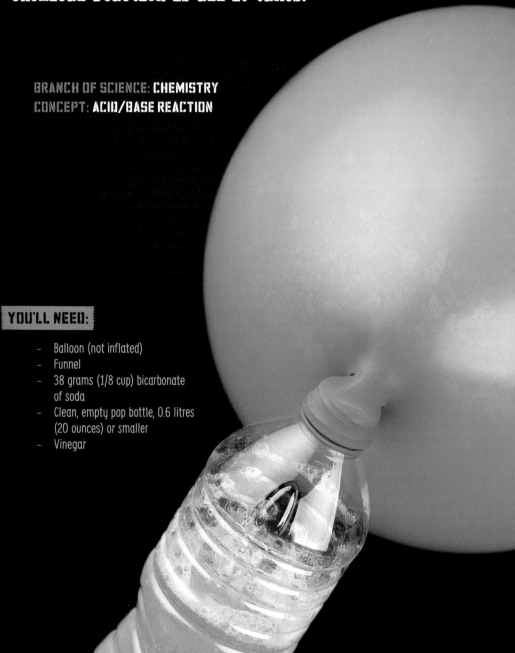

YOU'LL NEED:

- Balloon (not inflated)
- Funnel
- 38 grams (1/8 cup) bicarbonate of soda
- Clean, empty pop bottle, 0.6 litres (20 ounces) or smaller
- Vinegar

PUT IT TOGETHER:

STEP 1: Place the tip of the funnel inside the balloon.

STEP 2: Pour the bicarbonate of soda into the funnel. Shake the bicarbonate of soda into the balloon.

STEP 3: Add vinegar to the bottle until it's about half full.

STEP 4: Remove the funnel. Stretch the neck of the balloon over the top of the bottle. Make sure none of the bicarbonate of soda falls into the vinegar.

STEP 5: Hold the neck of the balloon tightly to the bottle. Tip the balloon to dump the bicarbonate of soda into the vinegar. What happens?

STEP 1   STEP 4

REUSABLE KNOWLEDGE:

Vinegar is an acid, and bicarbonate of soda is a base. Acids and bases react to make a new product. In this case, carbon dioxide gas is made. You can't always see a gas, but in this experiment the gas is easy to detect. It expands to fill the balloon. If you've ever made a cake, you've seen an acid and base reaction. Bubbles from reacting ingredients make the cake light and fluffy.

RECYCLING POP BOTTLES

Think you'd look good wearing pop bottles? How about using them to decorate your home? That's exactly where most recycled PET ends up. It is processed into many new materials including carpet fibre, T-shirt fabric, shoes and luggage. It is also used to make new PET containers for food and non-food products.

acid   sour tasting substance that reacts with a base

base   bitter tasting substance that reacts with an acid

VINEGAR ROCKET

A blasting rocket is an exciting experiment.
This rocket uses things you find around
your house. It packs a punch and explains an
important physics law.

BRANCH OF SCIENCE: PHYSICS
CONCEPT: NEWTON'S THIRD LAW OF MOTION

PUT IT TOGETHER:

STEP 1: Add vinegar to the bottle until it's 3/4 full. Put it aside.

STEP 2: Place the bicarbonate of soda in the centre of the toilet tissue. Carefully roll the tissue into a tight tube around the bicarbonate of soda.

STEP 3: Fold the ends over, and tape them in place to make a small packet. Make sure the packet is small enough to fit inside the mouth of the pop bottle.

STEP 4: Find an open area outside. Place the cardboard canister on the ground or prop it at an angle with bricks or rocks. Make sure the canister is not pointing towards people, animals or windows.

STEP 5: Drop the packet into the bottle. Quickly cork it. Put it cork side down inside the canister.

STEP 6: Back up several metres, and wait. It may take a little while for the rocket to take off. Do not go near it as you wait!

STEP 7: Find the landing place of your rocket. Then do the experiment again!

STEP 2

STEP 5

REUSABLE KNOWLEDGE:

This experiment shows Newton's Third Law of Motion. This law states that for every action there is an equal and opposite reaction. The vinegar and bicarbonate of soda reaction forms carbon dioxide. The carbon dioxide explodes backwards from the bottle. An equal force pushes the bottle forwards. This is the same principle that lifts rockets into space.

SUB IRRIGATED PLANTER

Do you like gardening? Are you sometimes afraid of watering your plants too little or too much? Try this project. It uses an important biology concept to keep plants watered just right.

BRANCH OF SCIENCE: BIOLOGY
CONCEPT: CAPILLARY ACTION

YOU'LL NEED:

- Clean, empty 2-litre bottle
- Ruler
- Marker pen
- Utility knife
- 3 strips of cotton from an old T-shirt, 2.5 centimetres wide x 10 centimetres (1 inch x 4 inches) long
- 700 grams (3 cups) potting soil
- Lettuce or herb seeds
- Water

SAFETY FIRST:

Ask an adult to help when using sharp tools such as a utility knife.

STEP 1: Make a mark 8 centimetres (3 inches) from the top of the bottle. Use the utility knife to cut a small "x" at this spot.

STEP 2: Repeat Step 1 to make a total of six small x's. Make them evenly spaced around the bottle 8 centimetres (3 inches) from the top.

STEP 3: Use the utility knife to cut off the top half of the bottle.

STEP 4: Turn the top upside down, and place it inside the bottom half.

STEP 5: Lay the fabric strips inside the top part of the bottle. They should extend through the neck of the bottle and touch the bottle's bottom.

STEP 6: Pack the soil around the cotton strips.

STEP 3

STEP 5

STEP 7: Plant seeds in the soil according to the package directions. Lightly water the seeds from the top.

STEP 8: Lift the top, and pour several centimetres of water into the bottle bottom. Replace the top.

STEP 9: Wait for your seeds to sprout and grow. Refill the bottom with water as needed.

REUSABLE KNOWLEDGE:

Like a straw, plant cells draw water and minerals upwards. This upward flow is called capillary action. Your waterer also uses capillary action. Water moves through openings in the cotton and soil to reach the plant's roots.

capillary action   ability of liquid to flow in small places against the force of gravity

LAVA LAMP

A lava lamp gives off a one-of-a-kind glow.
Its dancing blobs bring hours of enjoyment.
Make your own with this project. Then pride
yourself on knowing the science behind it.

BRANCH OF SCIENCE: CHEMISTRY
CONCEPT: OIL AND WATER IMMISCIBILITY

YOU'LL NEED:

- Clean, empty pop or water bottle (any size)
- Water
- Vegetable oil
- Food colouring (any colour)
- Effervescent tablets (Alka-Seltzer)
- Battery-operated tea light

PUT IT TOGETHER:

STEP 1: Add water to the bottle until it's 1/4 full.

STEP 2: Pour vegetable oil into the bottle until it is nearly full.

STEP 3: Drop 6 to 10 drops of food colouring into the bottle. Shake the bottle if needed to dissolve the food colouring.

STEP 4: Wait until the water and oil have separated. Place 1/4 of an effervescent tablet into the bottle. Watch the show!

STEP 5: When the bubbles stop, place another 1/4 tablet into the bottle. This time place the lit tea light upside down in the top of the bottle.

STEP 6: Take the lamp into a dark room for a lava lamp experience.

STEP 7: Add more tablets, 1/4 at a time, to keep the fun going.

STEP 4

REUSABLE KNOWLEDGE:

The oil and water don't mix together. Why? Water is much more dense than oil. Its molecules are more tightly packed together than oil's are. This makes water sink. The structure of the molecules is different for oil and water too. Water's molecules are polar, meaning they have a negative charge on one end and a positive charge on the other. Their charges hold the molecules to each other. Oil is nonpolar, without a charge, and doesn't mingle with the water molecules. The fizzing tablet releases gas. As the gas rises to the surface, it pulls coloured water with it. After the gas escapes, the water blobs sink back to the bottom of the bottle.

polar   molecule with one slightly positively charged and one slightly negatively charged end

nonpolar   uncharged molecule

COMPOSTING WORM FARM

Recycle more than a pop bottle with this project.
Recycle your kitchen scraps too. This project
does more than keep rubbish out of a landfill.
It improves the environment!

YOU'LL NEED:

- Clean, empty 2-litre bottle
- Utility knife
- 0.5-litre (16.9-ounce) water bottle
  filled with room temperature water
- Small scoop
- Ruler
- Sand
- Soil
- Fruit and vegetable peelings
- 0.12 litres (1/2 cup) of water
- 3 or 4 earthworms

SAFETY FIRST:

Ask an adult to help when using sharp tools such as a utility knife.

PUT IT TOGETHER:

STEP 1: Use the utility knife to cut the top off the 2-litre bottle. Cut it where the bottle starts to get narrower near the top. Discard the top.

STEP 2: Place the water bottle centred inside the 2-litre bottle. This will keep the worms near the outside of the bottle so you can watch them.

STEP 3: Carefully scoop about 2.5 centimetres (1 inch) of sand into the larger bottle. Make sure the water bottle stays in place.

STEP 4: Add about 2.5 centimetres (1 inch) of soil.

STEP 5: Add a layer of fruit and vegetable peelings.

STEP 6: Continue layering 2.5-centimetres (1-inch) layers of sand, soil and peelings. Stop when you reach about 5 centimetres (2 inches) from the top of the bottle.

STEP 2

STEP 5

STEP 7: Slowly pour water over the layers to make them slightly damp.

STEP 8: Add the worms.

STEP 9: Place the bottle in a cool, dark place.

STEP 10: Add small amounts of water every couple of days to keep the worm farm moist. Watch daily until the worms have composted all the scraps.

STEP 11: After several weeks, pour the newly composted soil and worms into a planter or flowerbed. Let them continue their work.

REUSABLE KNOWLEDGE:

Worms are nature's great recyclers. Worms turn food scraps and dead plants into rich soil fertilizer. As worms eat, their bodies change scraps into compost. They poop out this fertilizer to keep plants strong and healthy. Test out how well fertilizer works. Do plants grow better in composted soil or regular soil?

compost   breaks down fruits, vegetables and other materials to make soil better for gardening

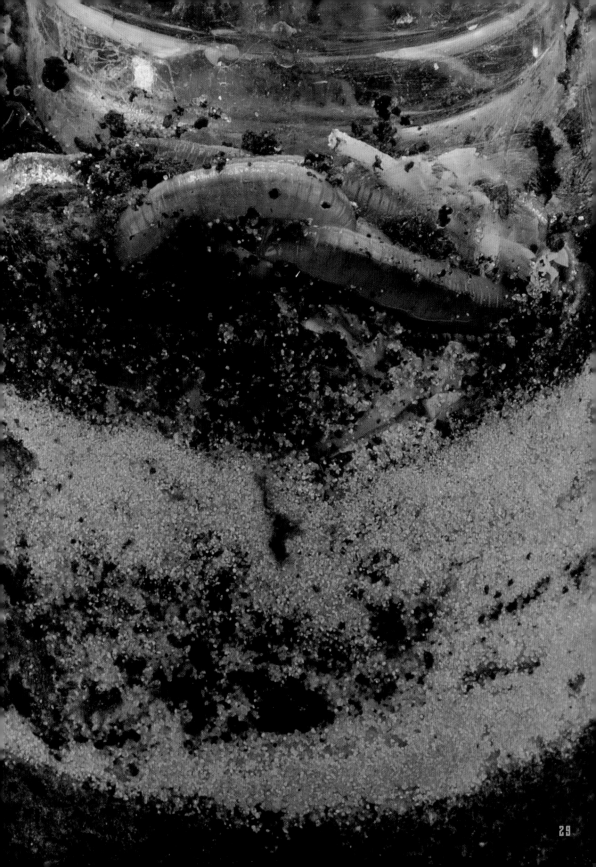

GLOSSARY

acid   sour tasting substance that reacts with a base

atmosphere   layer of gases surrounding Earth

atmospheric pressure   pressure caused by the weight of the atmosphere

base   bitter tasting substance that reacts with an acid

capillary action   ability of liquid to flow in small places against the force of gravity

cohesion   ability to stick together

compost   breaks down fruits, vegetables and other materials to make soil better for gardening

molecule   smallest particle of a substance with the properties of that substance

nonpolar   uncharged molecule

polar   molecule with one slightly positively charged and one slightly negatively charged end

surface tension   water 'skin'; water molecules form stronger bonds at the surface, causing the surface to act like a membrane

water vapour   water in its gaseous state

READ MORE

101 Great Science Experiments, Neil Ardley (DK Children, 2015)

365 Science Activities, Various (Usborne Publishing, 2014)

Big Book of Science Things to Make and Do, Rebecca Gilpin and Leonie Pratt
(Usborne Publishing, 2012)

Really Rotten Experiments (Horrible Science), Nick Arnold (Scholastic, 2014)

WEBSITES

www.bbc.co.uk/education/clips/zhbygk7
Does gas weigh anything? Find out in this video from BBC Bitesize.

www.bbc.co.uk/education/clips/zdhxpv4
Watch this video to see a homemade water rocket in action!

www.rigb.org/families/experimental
This website has lots of videos showing fun experiments you can do at home.

COMPREHENSION QUESTIONS

1. Describe the two concepts that cause bubbles to rise and drop back in the lava lamp project on p. 24.

2. Water is held inside an upside down bottle with a mesh window screen on p. 12. What term describes water's ability to do this?

3. Describe how a bottle dropped in a California, USA river might make its way to the Great Pacific Garbage Patch?

INDEX